AWAY FROM IT ALL BY UNDERGROUND

Trooping the Colour, by David Theyre Lee-Elliott, 1952

Published by Capital Transport Publishing Ltd
www.capitaltransport.com

Printed by Parksons Graphics

AWAY FROM IT ALL BY UNDERGROUND

Jonathan Riddell

Capital Transport

Contents

Away from it all by Underground at Whitsuntide, by M E M Law, 1932

Introduction

There have been a number of books on the subject of Underground posters, but these have mainly dealt with the large posters seen on walls inside and outside Underground stations. However there were also many smaller posters and these were often known as car cards or panel posters, and they were mainly designed to appear inside the vehicles themselves. These smaller posters have not previously been given the attention they deserve, even though the fame of their designers and the quality of their design can often equal that of the larger and better-known posters. This book hopes to go some way to correct this apparent omission by looking at some of these panel posters issued by London Transport and its predecessor, the Underground Group. More specifically, this book is concentrating on the 10x12 inch-sized panel posters mainly seen on Underground car draught screens. However, a few of the other longer car cards have also been included for comparison.

London Transport was created in 1933 by the amalgamation of several companies amongst which was the Underground Group. Until 1933 the Underground Group was the largest provider of public transport in London and the company controlled not only all of the Underground lines, with the exception of the Metropolitan Railway and the Southern Railway's Waterloo and City Line, but also most of the capital's buses and trams. So even though it was a completely new organisation it is, perhaps, correct to consider the new London Passenger Transport Board as being almost a continuation of the Underground Group with all the other companies absorbed into the new organisation. This is certainly true as far as its posters and corporate design were involved as the London Passenger Transport Board (known to all as London Transport) inherited a long and highly regarded history of art and design which had begun with the Underground Group back in 1908. This design heritage ranged from station architecture, its Johnston typeface (first introduced in 1916), signage and of course most importantly its posters. Much of this was down to one man, Frank Pick, who had joined the Underground Group in 1906. Two years later Pick was given responsibility for the company's publicity, even though he had no previous experience or qualifications in this field. At the time of his appointment the company's finances were in a bad way and one way of helping to improve this unfortunate state of affairs was to get more passengers by improving the quality and effectiveness of the company's advertising and corporate identity. Although Pick cannot claim to have single-handedly turned around the company's finances he was responsible for lifting the Underground's publicity to another, much higher level. When later he was to become the Managing Director of the Underground and then from 1933 Vice Chairman of London Transport he still retained a close interest in the pictorial posters that were commissioned. It has been said that Frank Pick was, perhaps, the most influential person in shaping the style of much of twentieth-century London, and the architectural and art historian Nikolaus Pevsner probably did not go too far when he described Pick as *"the greatest patron of the arts whom this century has so far produced in England, and indeed the ideal patron of our age"*. So, it is without a doubt that as a result of Pick's vision the Underground Group can be considered to have taken the lead in the development of commercial art and design.

When Pick joined the advertising Department of the Underground Group in 1908 he soon began to commission artists to design pictorial posters. Most, but not all, of these pictorial posters were of the standard double royal (40in x 25in) or double crown (30in x 20in) sizes which are still the standard format to be seen on station walls and the front of buses. It should not be considered surprising that the purpose of most of these pictorial posters was to encourage off-peak or leisure travel. Like most urban transport systems the primary function of the Underground was to enable Londoners to commute to and from work. As a result there were sharply defined peaks in the morning and afternoon rush hour and also on Saturday mornings when many still worked a half day. This meant that the Underground was an underused resource outside of the peaks and

at weekends and in need of more paying passengers. Frank Pick was well aware of this and saw the benefit of attempting to increase leisure travel to the financial benefit of the company. As has already been said, when Pick first started working for the Underground the company's finances were in a bad way and the Underground desperately needed to increase the number of passengers using it in order to increase its revenue. Fortunately, Frank Pick was the man to do this. Pick was aware that London was a large, quickly growing city and that many Londoners did not know the city well outside the area in which they lived. Frank Pick summed it up himself when he wrote: *"Another thing that seems to me so stupid is that here in London with unlimited opportunities no-one takes advantage of them at all. When I lived in York or Newcastle I was much better able to know what was moving in things than I am now when I am in London".*

With Pick's help the Underground Group was to change how Londoners saw London and open up the many attractions that were to be found in and beyond the city. Technological improvements in the vehicles played an important part in this as the early part of the twentieth century saw not just the introduction of the motorbus and electric tram but also a rapid growth in the Underground network. So when Pick took the opportunity to advertise London's many attractions as well as the surrounding towns, villages and countryside all of these could now be easily reached by the company's vehicles, and he was not just advertising the Underground and buses themselves but equally importantly London itself. Although much of this was due to the colourful posters which Pick commissioned to advertise the many attractions, the role of the bus, tram and Underground maps must not be forgotten. Issued in their hundreds of thousands they were the maps of London which many, if not most, people used for their travel around the city.

Not content with just using the full-size posters on the stations, small pictorial posters would increasingly appear inside vehicles be they bus, tram or Underground car. On the buses they would appear in the row of commercial adverts above the windows, likewise on the Underground vehicles. They might also appear at the end of the carriage. These small posters were often of equal artistic merit to the larger posters, and sometimes even surpassed them. Many of the same artists, such as Edward McKnight Kauffer, Tom Eckersley and Edward Bawden, whose work also appears on the double royal and double crown size posters, were also commissioned to design or illustrate the panel posters. That is not to say that on occasion certain artists appear to have been preferred for either one format or the other. The artist Tom Eckersley recalled that London Transport would sometimes try out a new artist on the smaller format and, if that was successful, a commission for a full-size poster would follow. It is not clear if he was thinking of himself. The reason for this uncertainty is because although in 1935 working with Eric Lombers he received his first commission from London Transport to design four panel posters they were also commissioned that year to illustrate six larger double royal size posters. However, in all of these latter cases the posters were mainly text with only a small illustration to add interest and catch the eye. Regardless as to whether the artist for these posters was well known or not these small posters could be used when the cost of a larger poster could not be justified. This resulted in certain subjects such as the Lord Mayor's Show and the Royal Tournament appearing more frequently in the smaller format than the larger double royal or double crown formats. However, there appeared to be no consistent rule as, for example, the Boat Race appeared regularly in both formats. Not all of these panel posters were used to promote leisure travel, although that was by far their most common function. Important developments in the Underground network were also advertised.

OPPOSITE:
This 1939 view of 1938 stock shows the position of London Transport panel posters on the glass draught screens. The posters are 'Wimbledon Championships' by Leonard Appelbee and 'Torchlight Tattoo', by Joy Williams.

At first most panel posters or car cards were in a relatively long and thin landscape format so that they could be posted inside the vehicles amongst the commercial advertising in the spaces above the windows. Other small posters in the vertical portrait format would be displayed at the ends of the railway carriages. However, by the late 1920s a slightly different size of panel poster was introduced. This being approximately 10.5in x 12in was of a much squarer format than those previously issued and soon became a very popular format for panel posters which were intended to be displayed on the draught screens to be found inside the sliding doors of the Underground carriages. It is perhaps worth noting that the use of the draught screens for displaying posters appears to have been reserved solely for those issued by the Company and not for commercial advertising. Occasionally panel posters in other sizes would also be displayed on the draught screens. Although originally intended to be displayed on the draught screens in the Underground cars this new size of panel poster would occasionally be posted elsewhere including station walls, but this use of these posters appears to be the exception to the rule and may not have been officially sanctioned.

The high-point of the art of the poster as far as London Transport and the Underground Group were concerned was clearly in the 1920s and 1930s. Pick himself admitted that when he first started to commission artists he was still finding his way. The outbreak of World War One did not see an immediate halt in the production of pictorial posters and it was during the War in 1915 that the man who was to become the Underground's most celebrated poster designer, Edward McKnight Kauffer, was first commissioned by Pick to design a poster. If there had not been an almost complete halt in the production of pictorial posters in 1917 and 1918 then it is likely that 1915 or 1916 would have been considered the start of Underground's Golden Age of posters, but the hiatus caused by the war meant it was not until 1920 that pictorial poster production was once again in full swing with talented artists such as Kauffer, Austin Cooper, Jean Dupas, Paul Nash, F Gregory Brown, Herry Perry and Dora M Batty being commissioned. Some of these artists, such as Kauffer, were primarily poster artists or graphic designers and made their name with the posters they designed for the Underground, whilst others whose work was more likely to be found in an art gallery were selected by Pick as he was keen to display their work across the Underground. A few, such as Edward Bawden, were a master of all fields. Most of the posters shown in this book come from this inter-war period, not just because that was when the best designs were to be found but also for the practical reason that after the Second World War the quantity of posters in all sizes and shapes was much reduced.

It is not surprising that, unlike the First World War, the Second World War saw an almost

OPPOSITE:
Interior view of 1931 standard-tube stock trailer car, for use on the Piccadilly line. In this standard-tube stock car Tom Purvis's poster for the British Industries Fair can be seen on two of the draught screens and illustrates that it was not just the 10in x 12in format panel posters that were used in this space, though these were much more common.

immediate halt in the production of pictorial posters encouraging off-peak travel to London's attractions. For the duration of the war any posters issued had to be part of the war effort since all the resources of London Transport were concentrated on providing a transport service in the very difficult wartime conditions. Rather than encouraging off-peak travel the main message nationwide was "Is your journey really necessary" and in London passengers were instructed how to behave so as to enable London's Tubes and buses to continue to provide a service for the benefit of all who needed to use them. By the end of the war London Transport's network was very run down and it would take time to make good the damage that had been inflicted upon it. It no longer had the ability to carry additional passengers which its pre-war posters encouraged. Instead, posters carried messages such as ones about the new extensions to the Central Line, rehabilitation of trains and reminders to passengers about the importance of courtesy in a campaign entitled 'Courtesy Aids Service'. The positioning of panel posters on the glass screens in Underground cars was not popular with the Underground's Chief Mechanical Engineer, William Graff-Baker, who took a close interest in all aspects of Underground train design and appearance, as was part of his duties. In a January 1947 memo to J H Brebner, then London Transport's Chief Public Relations Officer, he wrote:

"I have from time to time, I think, given some indication that I do not like the posters stuck on the windows of railway rolling stock. Some considerable trouble is taken, especially latterly, to obtain a good appearance in our cars and this is not improved by glass screens having paper notices stuck on them. Not only do these notices obscure the view and tend to cut the car into compartments to some extent, but, in practical effect can't be put up at all times with the neatness and regularity which should be observed in such a matter. I appreciate that the space in question is a very striking one and has considerable value for certain purposes, a value which is depreciated by constant use. It seems a long time since our screens were free of such notices. If, as I suppose, the spaces have an emergency value, clearly we cannot now the war is over be in such a constant state of emergency as to warrant any but the most exceptional use of this space. I appreciate that it is a question of relative values, which I am perhaps, ill-qualified to judge from a publicity point of view, and while I would not in any sense wish to depreciate the value of the "Courtesy Aids Service" campaign, I hardly think it constitutes such an emergency of the type I envisage as to warrant the use of the railway car screens for posters on this matter....".

By the time this memo was sent the number of posters produced had already decreased dramatically, as had the use of glass screens as sites for posters and probably, regardless of this memo, the decline in their appearance on glass screens was inevitable. Even so, within a few years London Transport's pictorial posters once again began to encourage off-peak travel. Post-war London was, however, very different to pre-war London and this can be reflected in the style and number of pictorial posters that London Transport issued. Would this change have been so great if Pick was still in post? It is hard to say, but it was not long before the post-war style of poster took on its own identity, even though it was still constrained by the same range of poster sizes. With just a handful of pictorial posters being issued each year in the 1950s, 60s and 70s very few would be panel posters of the type shown in this book. Indeed, as far as is known the last pictorial panel poster in this 10in x 12in format was that by Peter Roberson in 1969 for the Lord Mayor's Show. This was not, however, the last pictorial panel poster to be issued, as Peter Roberson continued to produce poster designs for the Lord Mayor's Show but in a slightly different size.

OPPOSITE:
Two panel posters can be seen displayed on the draught screens. That on the left is the 'Presentation of Colours by HM the King', by Dora M Batty, whilst that on the right is for the Davis Cup, Wimbledon, by Walter Goetz.

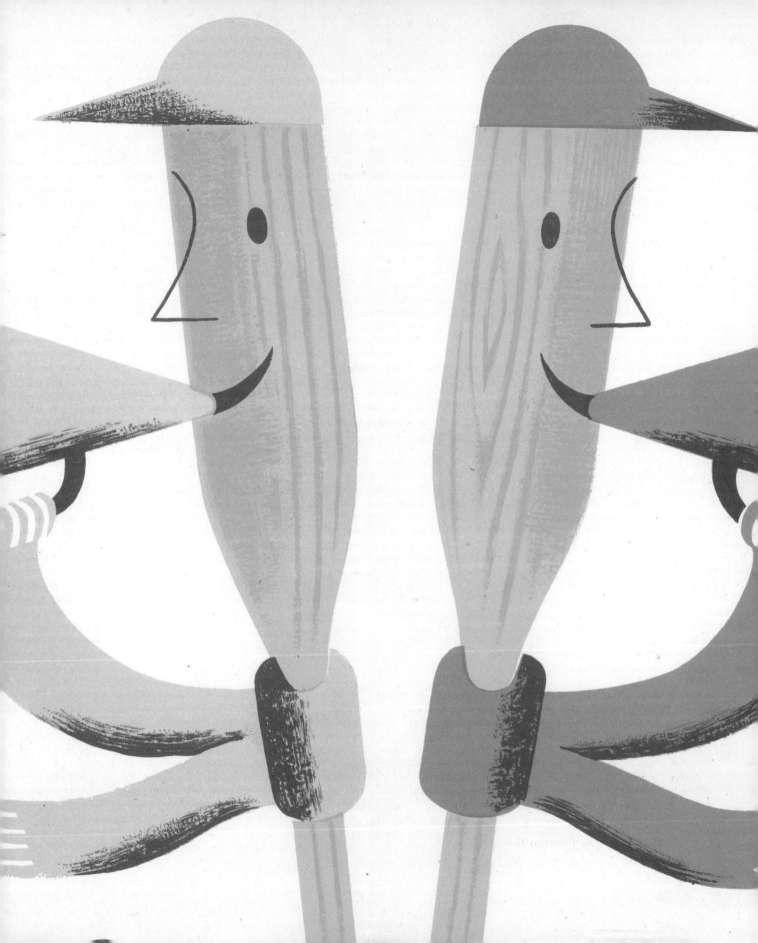

Boat Race

The annual Boat Race between Oxford and Cambridge universities remains one of the most famous sporting fixtures to be found in London even though few spectators would have attended either of the two universities. Held in March or early April the race's four mile and 374 yard long course along the River Thames runs from Putney to Mortlake giving ample opportunity for the 250,000-plus spectators who line the River Thames each year to watch the race. In the 1920s and 1930s even the pre-race practice days were considered an attraction, with these days also advertised on the company's letterpress posters. The race's enduring popularity was no doubt due in part to the fact that unlike all the other major sporting events in London there was no need to buy a ticket to watch it and so the race could be viewed freely by anyone able to get to the Thames. Before television this was the best, though not the only way, to see it. Some races were filmed by British Pathé and even when the Boat Race was first televised in 1938 few could have taken advantage, as by the outbreak of the war in 1939 television was estimated to reach only 25,000 to 40,000 homes. Whilst most of those attending the event would have reached the river by Tube, bus or tram the Southern Railway also had several stations nearby, and in 1938 and 1939 London Transport's Boat Race posters unusually included these Southern Railway stations as well as its own Underground stations on its pictorial panel posters. The Boat Race was suspended for the duration of the Second World War and did not appear on a London Transport poster again until 1951. The other race which appears on some of London Transport's posters is the annual Head of the River Race. This was founded in 1925. It is not nearly so well known as the Boat Race and for this reason never justified its own pictorial posters. Although in the 1920s and 1930s it did share with the Boat Race some of the Underground's letterpress posters it was not until the 1950s that it appeared on some of the pictorial panel posters advertising the Oxford and Cambridge Boat Race. This was the last decade in which the Boat Race was so heavily promoted by London Transport since, with the exception of a pictorial poster issued in 1990, the last panel poster to advertise the race was issued in 1959.

BOAT RACE
SAT. MARCH 21

▸ NEAREST STATIONS ◂
PUTNEY BRIDGE
HAMMERSMITH
RAVENSCOURT PK
TURNHAM GREEN
CHISWICK PARK

C BVRTON

LONDON TRANSPORT

Nearest stations
PUTNEY BRIDGE
HAMMERSMITH
RAVENSCOURT PK.
TURNHAM GREEN
CHISWICK PARK

Bus routes
9. 11. 14. 22. 27. 30
32. 33. 55. 73. 74. 85
93. 96. 127. 173
255. 273. 291. 373

Tram routes
26. 28. 30. 57. 63
67. 89

BOAT RACE MARCH 17 - 2.30

Boat Race April 6th 2.45pm, by Herry Perry, 1935
In contrast to the posters by Anna Zinkeisen and Charles Burton (shown opposite) in which the focus of attention is on the spectators, Herry Perry has chosen to ignore the spectators and concentrate instead on the two boats themselves.

OPPOSITE:
Boat Race, by Charles Burton, 1931
The elegant style of this poster is enhanced by the attractive hand-drawn lettering with no corporate roundel or Johnston lettering in sight.

Boat Race, by Anna Zinkeisen, 1934
Better known for her murals for the Cunard liners Queen Mary and Queen Elizabeth, Anna Zinkeisen designed 18 panel posters for London Transport in 1934. In this poster although no boats are shown the outline of Hammersmith Bridge is clearly recognisable. In this poster the two teams are represented by the opposing pairs of women supporters in the light blue of Cambridge and dark blue of Oxford.

Wednesday, March 24 · 11 o'clock

STATIONS
Hammersmith
Ravenscourt Park
Stamford Brook · Turnham Gn.
Chiswick Park · Putney Bridge

37. 471. 14000

DRAKE BROOKSHAW.

Boat Race, by Percy Drake Brookshaw, 1937
This was the artist's second Underground poster for the Boat Race, the first being issued in 1928.
He was not commissioned to design another poster for London Transport until 1958.

OPPOSITE:

Boat Race, by Walter Goetz, 1936
Although this format of poster was intended for display inside Underground cars it did not mean
that they only had to promote travel by Underground as can be seen in this poster by Goetz.
This is the only pictorial poster for the Boat Race to only advertise travel by tram and trolleybus
rather than the Underground. Of course, if travelling by London Transport, some destinations
such as the Aldershot Tattoo, could only be reached by private bus or coach hire. In 1936 alone
several posters in this format were issued to promote LT's services in general without reference
to any particular mode of travel.

100th Boat Race, by Ian Ribbons, 1954

It should be noted that 100th Boat Race did not mean that it was the 100th Anniversary of the Boat Race as the race was not held during the two world wars. The first of these university boat races took place in 1829, but it was not established as a regular annual event until 1856.

OPPOSITE:

Boat Race, by Tom Eckersley, 1951

Usually only five or six Underground stations were included as being convenient for the Boat Race but on this poster Gunnersbury and Kew Gardens stations were added to make eight stations listed. This reverted to seven stations in 1952 and five in 1953.

Boat Race, by Tom Eckersley, 1953

Although the main title "Boat Race" clearly refers to the Oxford and Cambridge Boat Race this poster also advertises the lesser known Head of the River Race.

Cricket

The game of cricket was and still is one of England's most popular sports and its two most famous grounds are both situated in London. Lord's cricket ground, which lies in the north of London, is home to Middlesex County Cricket Club and, on the south bank, The Oval is home to Surrey County Cricket Club. It is an interesting fact that neither club is now based in the county of their name since in 1965 the County of Middlesex was abolished, most of it becoming part of Greater London. Similarly, over the years, those parts of Surrey nearest to London have also been absorbed into London rather than remaining as Surrey.

Both Lord's and The Oval cricket grounds had stations with the same name as the cricket grounds and were easily accessible by the Underground. Although in the case of Lord's station it was soon to close and was replaced the same day by a new St John's Wood station on the Stanmore branch of the Bakerloo Line, now the Jubilee Line. For some unknown reason it was only from the late 1920s that the Underground regularly issued pictorial posters advertising cricket matches at these two major sporting venues. This continued throughout the 1930s. The seven panel posters shown here all advertise travel to the International Test Matches which were held at Lord's or The Oval cricket grounds. Whilst this was to be the main form of cricket to appear on these panel posters other posters were issued from time to time listing the numerous county matches which were also regularly played at both of these grounds. With the exception in 1938 of a poster advertising both the Oxford versus Cambridge and Eton versus Harrow cricket matches, which were held at Lord's, it was only the Test Matches that appeared on pictorial panel posters. When county matches were advertised on posters the poster did not advertise just one match but would list a whole series of matches that were to be found at cricket grounds around London. These posters were usually in the larger Double Crown and Double Royal formats. The reason behind only Test Matches having their own poster may have been that London Transport considered only these International Test matches important enough to justify their own poster, or it may have been that there were too many county matches for each to have its own poster and that a larger poster allowed more matches, sometimes up to fourteen to be listed at the same time. After the Second World War London Transport did not produce another pictorial poster for cricket until 1951 and this time it listed many grounds some as far afield as Guildford and Tunbridge Wells.

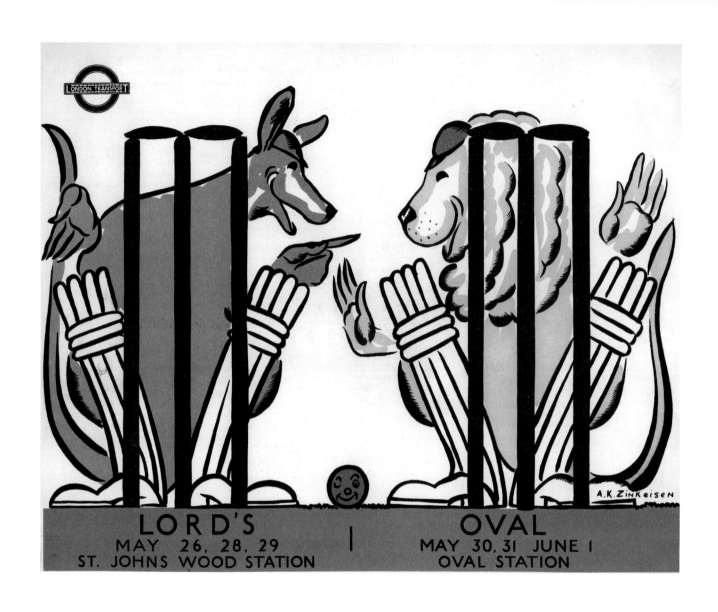

LORD'S
MAY 26, 28, 29
ST. JOHNS WOOD STATION

OVAL
MAY 30, 31 JUNE 1
OVAL STATION

Lord's; Oval, by Anna Zinkeisen, 1934
No need to name the countries playing. The kangaroo and the lion say it all.

Lord's; England v South Africa, by Herry Perry, 1935
Whether the rhebok would have been as much associated with the visiting team's country as the kangaroo was for Australia is questionable.

At the Oval, by Dooley, 1935
Although not stated on the poster this test match was between South Africa and England.

England v New Zealand at Lord's, by Gill Lancaster, 1937
This design by Gill Lancaster was also used that year on a poster advertising cricket at Lord's.

THIRD TEST MATCH · THE OVAL

ENGLAND v WEST INDIES

AUGUST 19 21 22

Station **OVAL** or by bus or tram

England v West Indies, by Clifford Ellis and Rosemary Ellis, 1939
In this poster for The Oval, Clifford and Rosemary Ellis have chosen to focus attention on the
fielder attempting to catch the ball, but cleverly leaving the outcome still in some doubt.

First Test Match; Lords, by Clifford Ellis and Rosemary Ellis, 1939
This is one of the few posters issued by London Transport for travel to Lord's Station. The
reason is simple, because on 11th June 1939 the Metropolitan Line's St John's Wood
Underground Station was renamed Lord's only to be closed permanently a few months later on
19th November 1939. As new it had been intended that this newly named station would open for
the major match days at the cricket ground but the onset of the Second
World War led to its permanent closure.

Exhibitions and Shows

As befitting the capital city, London has had several major exhibition halls, the best known being White City, Olympia, the Royal Agricultural Halls and Earls Court. Over the years these have housed a wide variety of events ranging from cattle shows to the Ideal Home Exhibition. Whilst many of the more important events held at these major exhibition spaces were regularly advertised on pictorial posters, other events were only occasionally advertised by London Transport posters. The exact reasons why some events justified a poster and others did not is not known. Of course the popularity of some of these events would appear to be the justification for issuing a poster but other events such as the Exhibition of Modern Silverwork, though no doubt popular, would have a much lesser appeal to the public and there may be other reasons for supporting this event with a poster.

However, one annual event that was regularly advertised on panel posters from 1928 to 1939 was The British Industries Fair. The aim of the Fair was to encourage production by British firms and the success of the first Fair led to it becoming an almost annual event until 1957. From 1920 there was also an exhibition for heavy industries in Birmingham. The London sections changed venues several times but by 1938 it had settled on Olympia and the newly opened Earls Court building. By 1948 the purpose of the British Industries Fair was described by M Logan in *The Histories of the Fair* as being 'to show the world the strength of British industry, the craftsmanship, the design and the quality that is implied in the words British Made'.

Another colourful event that surprisingly appeared on only three posters was the Chelsea Flower Show. Held in the grounds of the Chelsea Hospital since 1913 this was, and still is, a popular annual event in the London calendar and with its colourful nature should have been an ideal choice as the subject for several London Transport posters. It is not known why it appeared so rarely but maybe it being an eleven minute walk away from the nearest Underground station at Sloane Square made it a less attractive subject for London Transport to advertise, though of course several buses did pass nearby.

BRITISH INDUSTRIES FAIR
WHITE CITY. FEB. 20 — MARCH 2.
BOOK TO WOOD LANE. TUBE STATION.

C BURTON

BRITISH INDUSTRIES FAIR
OLYMPIA FEB. 17TH TO 28TH.
HAMMERSMITH · WEST KENSINGTON
BARONS COURT OR ADDISON ROAD

UNDERGROUND

EXHIBITION OF

JULY 4 TO 16

MODERN SILVERWORK
GOLDSMITHS' HALL
FOSTER LANE E C 2
10AM-7·30PM   ADMISSION FREE
NEAREST STATIONS
ST. PAULS AND MANSION HOUSE

The Baynard Press, London

Exhibition of Modern Silverwork, by Edward McKnight Kauffer, 1938
This was the First Exhibition of Modern Silverwork to be held at Goldsmith's Hall and is, perhaps, a surprising subject to be considered important enough for a poster by such a famous artist. This, exhibition appears to have been so popular that Kauffer's image was also used on a second Underground poster advertising the extension of the exhibition by another week.

OPPOSITE:
British Industries Fair, by Edward McKnight Kauffer, 1928
Although advertising the British Industries Fair, and by implication everything British made, it is perhaps a little ironic that this poster was by the noted American poster artist who made his name designing posters for the Underground and as a result became Britain's leading poster designer during the 1920s and 1930s.

British Industries Fair, by Charles Burton, 1929
In 1929 Charles Burton was commissioned to design this poster advertising the 1930 British Industries Fair. Burton went on to design several more very stylish posters for London Transport over the next few years.

DAILY MAIL IDEAL HOME EXHIBITION

OLYMPIA   APRIL 5-30

NEAREST STATIONS

ADDISON ROAD · WEST KENSINGTON · BARONS COURT

NOV.
2-26
I'6 ALL DAY

WOMAN'S FAIR · OLYMPIA
STATIONS · ADDISON ROAD · WEST KENSINGTON
BARONS COURT —— OR BY BUS OR COACH

Radiolympia, by Klara, 1939

Radiolympia was the high point of the radio enthusiast's year, a fact not lost on the radio magazines, which published bumper editions for the show. The first National Radio Exhibition was held at Olympia in September 1926. It was only after the popularity of the show in 1934 with its 238,000 visitors that London Transport began to issue an annual poster for this event. This poster by Klara was the last London Transport poster to advertise Radiolympia as the event was cancelled for the war years.

OPPOSITE:
Daily Mail Ideal Home Exhibition, unknown, 1938

Woman's Fair, unknown, 1938

This show with its seven sections on the home, children, food, fashion, beauty, careers and leisure claimed to be the first to cover "every possible interest of women". The show lost money for its organisers and it is very unlikely that future shows would have been held even without the onset of the Second World War the following November.

Cruft's Dog Show, by Herry Perry, 1937
The world famous Cruft's dog show started as far back as 1891, but it was not until 1937 that London Transport issued its only pictorial poster advertising the show. Two years later the show was taken over by the Kennel Club.

Kennel Club Show, by Tom Eckersley and Eric Lombers, 1938
A year after issuing its first ever poster for Cruft's, London Transport issued its one and only poster for the Kennel Club Show. This may have been an attempt by London Transport to appear even-handed in promoting these two competing events.

International Horse Show, Olympia, by Charles Burton, 1930

From 1907 until 1939 the International Horse Show was a major event in London's calendar and as such featured on several Underground panel posters. Mounties must have featured strongly in the Show that year, because although Burton's poster showing three Canadian Mounties jumping their horses over the roof of Olympia was the only Underground poster to advertise that year's show another poster by Cecil Aldin was also commissioned, either by the venue or the Show itself, and this too portrayed a Mountie. Another major Horse Show was held at Richmond for seventy-five years and this too features on many Underground posters in the 1920s and 1930s.

OPPOSITE:

Chelsea Flower Show, by Reimann School T V Y, 1938

In 1938 five designs for panel posters were commissioned from the Reimann School, which was the first commercial art school in Britain. These appear to have been designed by three different artists known only by their initials. T V Y who designed this poster also produced another for the Smithfield Club Cattle Show.

Chelsea Flower Show, by Klara, 1939

Hungarian designer Klara provided posters for the Underground between 1935 and 1939.

CHELSEA
FLOWER
SHOW

MAY 25·26·27

STATION   SLOANE SQUARE
BUSES   11 · 39 · 46 · 137
COACH   K3

CHELSEA
FLOWER *Show*

MAY 17 18 19
STATION SLOANE SQUARE BUSES 11,39,46,137 COACH K3

Football

Football is the most popular sport in England and London is home not just to several of the country's leading teams but also to Wembley, modern home of the Football Association Cup Final. It is, therefore, no surprise that the Underground Group and later London Transport between them issued more posters advertising football matches than for any other sporting event.

Many of these posters consisted just of text and no image, or perhaps just a small image above the list of clubs to catch the eye. This was all that was needed as most fans were regular supporters and would know the way to their club. They would not need a colourful poster to encourage them to travel by Tube, bus or tram to support one of the many football matches to be found every Saturday during the season, unless perhaps it was an away match. This still left plenty of matches which justified a pictorial poster.

In the 1920s and 1930s these were usually important matches such as the Cup Final or an International match. However, the first pictorial posters advertising football that were issued by the Underground appeared before the First World War in 1913. More followed in 1914 and then there was a gap of several years until in 1923 the Cup Final moved to Wembley.

It is hard to believe today that when plans for the British Empire Exhibition at Wembley were being considered some felt that it was too far from central London for such a major exhibition site. A year before the British Empire Exhibition of 1924 to 1925 opened, the Empire Stadium as Wembley Stadium was then known was already complete and ready for the 1923 FA Cup Final. On the day of the first Cup Final a new Wembley Stadium station also opened but it was not served by Underground trains. This did not matter to the Underground as there were up to five stations which it recommended fans travelling to Wembley to use. Wembley became the Cup Final's permanent home and that year the Underground began issuing an annual panel poster for the FA Cup Final rather than just more general posters for football.

These panel posters continued to be issued from 1923 up to the start of the Second World War. However, not all posters for the Cup Final were issued by the Underground Group as the Metropolitan Railway, a separate company until becoming part of London Transport in 1933, also issued a number of colourful posters advertising travel by its electric trains to Wembley Park station.

Cup Final, by André Edouard Marty, 1933
This unusual view of the Cup Final completely ignores the thrills, action and
excitement that supporters would hope to see. However, it is typical of Marty's style as can be
seen from other posters by him throughout the book.

OPPOSITE:
To the Cup Final, by L B Black, 1925
Black's viewpoint at ground level from one goalpost to the other is unique and striking.

Cup Final, by Charles Burton, 1930
Rather than concentrate on the action of the match Burton has cleverly decided to emphasise the
anticipation and excitement as the fans watch one of the teams enter on to the pitch.

Cup Final, by Anna Zinkeisen, 1934
Effective as it may be, this dramatic view of two players reaching for the ball with the cheering fans in the background clearly makes no attempt to portray a realistic view of a match at Wembley as the Stadium is completely missing, with the cheering fans standing on the edge of the pitch. Also lacking on this poster is any advice as to how supporters should travel to Wembley, be it by Underground, bus or tram or train.

ENGLAND v. GERMANY

2·30 DEC·4

ECKERSLEY LOMBERS

TOTTENHAM HOTSPUR
FOOTBALL GROUND

Station—Manor House, thence tram 27, 59 or 79
Buses 39, 69 & 76.   Trams 27, 39, 49, 59, 71 & 79

England v. Germany, by Tom Eckersley and Eric Lombers, 1935
This was the first full international match to be played between these two countries in England
and was held amidst much controversy as that year the anti-Semitic Nuremberg Laws had just
come into effect, the Versailles Treaty ignored and the Luftwaffe formed.
Even with this background the match passed off peacefully with the result:
England 3, Germany 0.

Cup Final, by Herry Perry, 1935
If one looks closely one can see that the footballers and their kit are made out of genuine
London Transport bell punch bus tickets which the artist must have acquired for the purpose.

OPPOSITE:
Cup Final, May 1st, by G R Morris, 1937
This poster takes an unusual viewpoint on the Cup Final, showing not the footballers, the match
or even the spectators but the less glamourous preparation before the day itself.

Cup Final, April 30th, by Tom Eckersley and Eric Lombers, 1938
This appears to be the last panel poster issued by London Transport for the Cup Final.

CUP FINAL   **MAY 1ST**

STATIONS : Alperton, thence bus 83 ; Wembley Park ; Wembley Wembley Hill or Wembley Stadium   TROLLEYBUS : 662
BUSES : 11 · 18 · 18ᶜ · 83 ; also special service Aldwych to Wembley

37. 1837.1 IM.   VINCENT BROOKS, DAY & SON, LTD., LONDON W.C. 2.

CUP FINAL APRIL 30

UNDERGROUND to Wembley, Wembley Park, Alperton thence bus 83, Wembley Hill or Wembley Stadium.   TROLLEYBUS 662
BUS 11 · 18 · 18ᶜ or 83, also special service Aldwych to Wembley

30.406.25,000   Curwen Press

AMICITIAM TRAHIT AMOR

Lord Mayor's Show

The first pictorial poster to advertise The Lord Mayor's Show appeared back in 1909 and since then the Underground Group and London Transport have continued to issue either a letterpress or pictorial poster almost every year for this important event which is unique to London. The Lord Mayor's Show which is officially listed in the City's Civic Calendar as 'The Procession to the Royal Courts of Justice and Presentation of the Lord Mayor to the Chief Justices' is one of the longest running events in London's calendar since the office of Lord Mayor of the City of London (not to be confused with the Mayor of London) dates from 1189. On starting his term as Lord Mayor it was a requirement that the Mayor travelled to Westminster to present himself to the monarch's representatives, to take an oath of loyalty to the Sovereign. Over the years pageantry and display gradually grew up around this event so that by the 16th century it was firmly established as a major entertainment for Londoners.

From 1751 to 1959 The Lord Mayor's Show was held on the 9th November, only then moving to the second Saturday in November to lessen the traffic congestion caused by holding it on weekdays. It was one of the few events that continued to take place without interruption right through the Second World War. Until 1952 the route varied each year so that it could pass through the Lord Mayor's home ward.

Over the years the number of participants has increased dramatically and includes bands and members of privileged regiments of the City of London such as The Royal Regiment of Fusiliers and the Honourable Artillery Company. Privileged regiments have the right to march through the City with bayonets fixed, colours flying, and drums beating. The many other participants lend a unique and colourful flavour to the occasion and usually include organisations that the Lord Mayor wishes to support or has belonged to before becoming Lord Mayor, such as charities, schools and business associations.

Each year the procession begins at the Guildhall where the Lord Mayor receives, together with the new Sheriff, personal gifts from a restricted group of relevant City institutions, usually including the Lord Mayor's own Livery Company and Ward Club. Then after a breakfast The Lord Mayor is escorted to his or her coach in Guildhall Yard by the Court of Aldermen and is driven off to Mansion House which is the official residence of the Lord Mayor. There the Lord Mayor waits for the show to pass from the terrace. The parade begins about 11am and finishes around 3:30pm. Whilst the procession is over three miles long the route itself is much shorter.

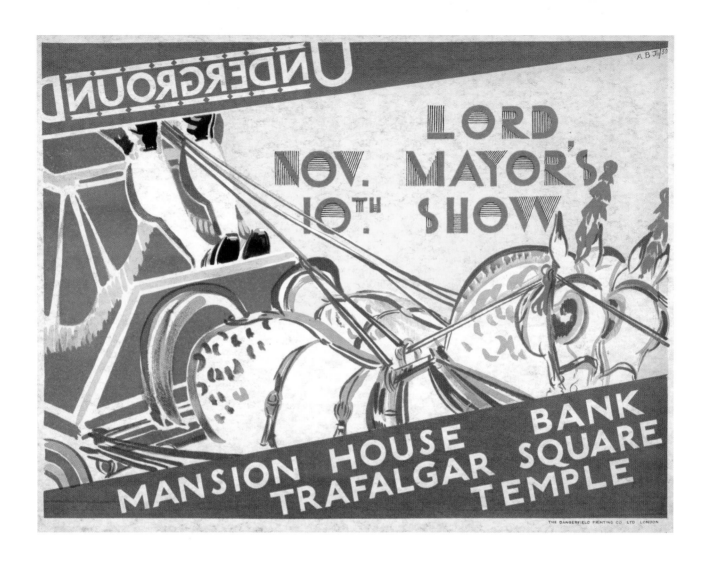

Lord Mayor's Show, by Arnrid Johnston, 1930
Until 1959 the Show was regularly held on 9th November each year. From that year, to reduce
traffic problems, the date was altered to the second Saturday in November. The reversed
Underground name at the top of the poster conveys a sense of coming out from a station to see
the Show and seeing the logotype from behind.

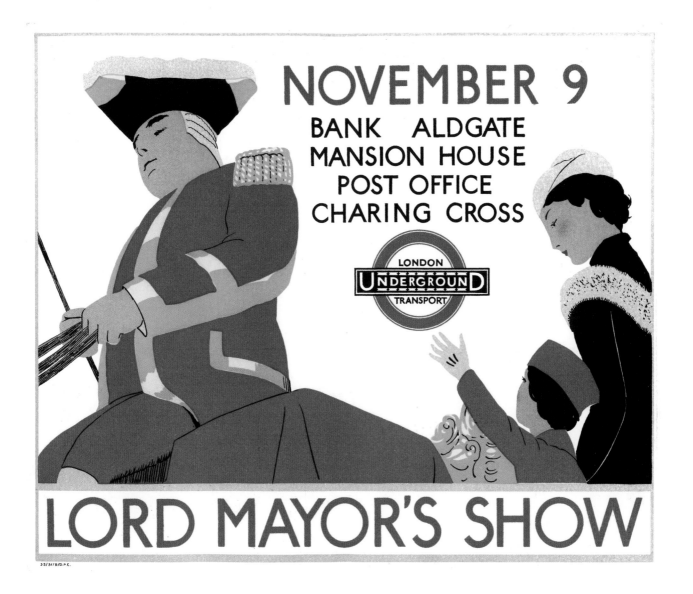

Lord Mayor's Show, by André Edouard Marty, 1933
In order to capture the atmosphere of the Lord Mayor's Show Marty has cleverly chosen to show just the coachman driving the Lord Mayor's coach and not the coach itself, such a symbol of the procession, or even the Lord Mayor himself. It is driven past a cheering girl and her mother: a signature feature of Marty's posters of this era.

Lord Mayor's Show, by Anna Zinkeisen, 1934
Surprisingly, on this as on several other posters advertising the Lord Mayor's Show, there is no information as to which Underground stations are the closest to the route.

Lord Mayor's Show, by Herry Perry, 1935
Today, there are 110 livery companies and this poster shows the coats of arms of six of these,
amongst which can be seen the Worshipful Company of Gold and Silver Wyre Drawers, the
Worshipful Company of Grocers and the Worshipful Company of Fishmongers.

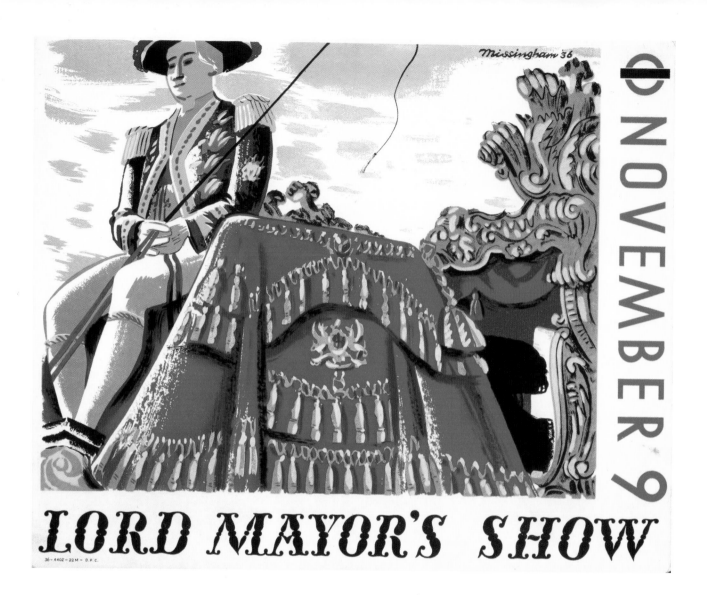

Lord Mayor's Show, by Harold Missingham, 1936
This was one of three panel posters designed by the Australian artist Harold (Hal) Missingham.
After the war he became the Director of the Art Gallery of New South Wales which under his
leadership made an outstanding contribution to Australian contemporary art.

Lord Mayor's Show, by Edward Wadsworth, 1936

London Transport commissioned two Lord Mayor's Show panels in 1936. This poster by
the celebrated artist Edward Wadsworth was printed, but not used. It is possible that the
image of the two guns was not considered appropriate for such a celebratory event.

Motor, Motorcycle and Cycle Shows

The Underground's first poster to advertise a motor show appeared in 1908. It had no image, just the words "UNDERGROUND Book Here for Angel (Agricultural Hall Station) for the Motor Show". It was not until 1928 that the Underground began to issue annual posters for the Olympia Motor Show. These continued to be issued until 1938. No poster was issued in 1939 as by the time of the show the Second World War had already started.

The Olympia Motor Show was a very popular event, with many, no doubt, wishing to view what they could not afford. At the time car ownership was mainly the preserve of the wealthy but even so the number of private cars on the roads doubled during the 1930s from a remarkable one to two million by the outbreak of the First World War. Why it took so long for the Underground to advertise this very popular event is not known as its history went back to 1896 when Britain's first motor show was held at the Imperial Institute under the auspices of Lawson's Motor Car Club. The first British International Motor Show (different from the one advertised at the Agricultural Halls) was held in 1903 at Crystal Palace before moving in 1904 to Olympia and then again in 1937 to Earls Court where it remained for 40 years with the exception of the war years.

Another associated event which London Transport issued several panel posters for was the Motorcycle and Cycle Show. To gain an idea of its importance it is perhaps best to read a contemporary account from the December 1933 issue of the Motorcyclist Magazine: *"The Motor Cycle Show is back at Olympia. Last year, what with the industrial depression and all, the manufacturers decided to let this annual fixture stand over for the first time since Great War days, but on November 25th the exhibition opened once again. ... The British Show is the most important of its kind in the world. It would be curious if it were not. .....It is also an event in London life. Olympia itself, the building, is the finest exhibition hall that we have and considered as a spectacle alone the Show beats the Paris Salon and the other continental fixtures, and does so pretty easily. The Minister of Transport himself was to open the Show, and among the visitors was expected to be H.R.H. the Duke of Gloucester. Prince Henry, as he is still sometimes called, is the third son of H.M. The King, and, like his brothers, has run a motorcycle of his own."*

MOTOR SHOW

OLYMPIA
OCT.15th–24th

WEST KENSINGTON, BARONS COURT or ADDISON RD.

UNDERGROUND

JENNER

1884/9·31

The Baynard Press

C BURTON

MOTOR SHOW
OLYMPIA OCT 16th–25th

WEST KENSINGTON – HAMMERSMITH or ADDISON Rᵈ STATION

1755/4000/9·9·30

THE DANGERFIELD PRINTING CO. LTD. LONDON

Motor Show, by Dorothy Paton, 1929

The Motor Show roundel which dominates this poster cleverly combines the traditional Underground roundel used for station nameplates with a tyre representing the motorcar thus reinforcing the message to visit the Show by Underground.

OPPOSITE:

Motor Show, by Jenner, 1931

In this poster Jenner cleverly uses the car's two nearside wheels, plus the spare, to form each letter O of the words "Motor Show".

Motor Show, Olympia October 16 - 25th, by Charles Burton, 1930

Most of the posters only show the larger, more expensive and mainly unaffordable cars. In this poster cars from both ends of the market are shown. Whilst the gentleman studies the smaller more affordable car, the lady appears to be admiring the size and luxury of the other grander vehicle.

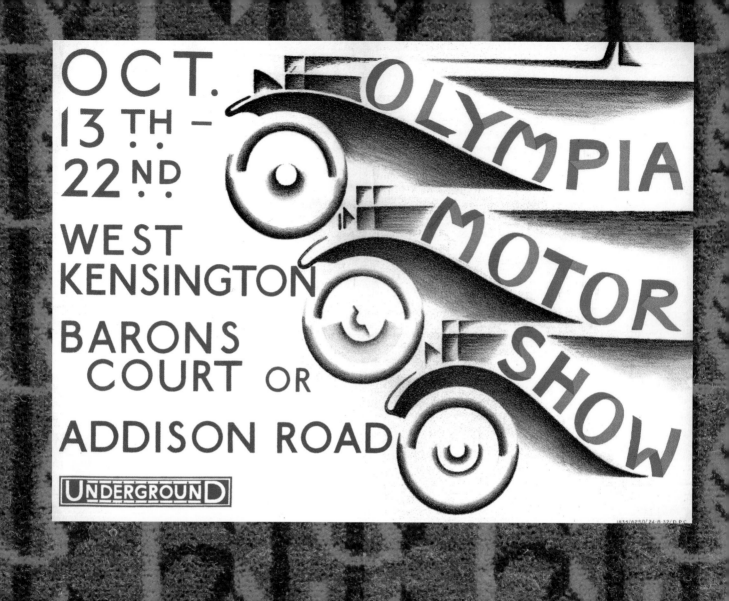

Olympia Motor Show, by André Edouard Marty, 1933
This portrayal of a woman driving along an empty road between green fields to Olympia bears little resemblance to the truth. Olympia was in urban west London and the roads would not have been so empty with, it is claimed, one million cars on the road by this time. Indeed the following year, 1934, saw the highest ever numbers of road casualties with 7,343 deaths and 231,603 injuries, due in part to the 1930 Road Traffic Act which abolished all speed limits for cars.

OPPOSITE:
Olympia Motor Show, by Vera Willoughby, 1932
In 1932 Vera Willoughby designed seven panel posters for the Underground.

Motor Show, by Herry Perry, 1935
In this poster Herry Perry has altered the proportions of the London Transport roundel so that it
becomes the front wheel of the car.

Motor Show, Olympia, by Anna Zinkeisen, 1934
Anna Zinkeisen's stylised car with huge curved wheel arches sums up the prevailing design of the
era which was in full streamline moderne mode.

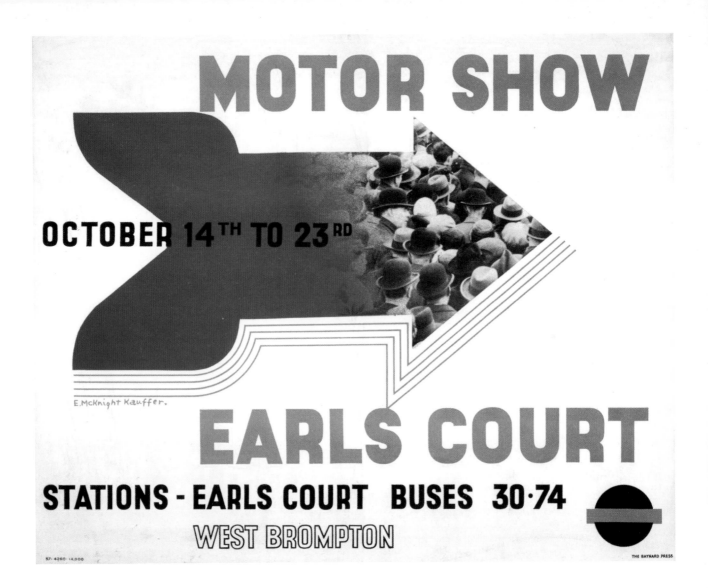

Motor Show, Earls Court, by Edward McKnight Kauffer, 1937
In 1937 this panel poster and a full size double royal poster, both by Edward McKnight Kauffer,
were issued. This was the only year in which a full size poster was also issued for this event.

OPPOSITE:
Cycle and Motor Cycle Show, by Charles Burton, 1930
Perhaps a sign of the times, as in none of these posters is a woman shown driving a motorbike.
They are either riding pillion or shown on the bicycle. Contrast this with the posters for the Motor
Show where the only driver shown is a woman.

Motor Cycle and Cycle Show, by Herry Perry, 1931
Was it a conscious decision by the artist to put the lady on the bicycle in Edwardian dress and the
motorcyclist and his passenger in a contemporary 1930 style, thus suggesting that the bicycle
was yesterday's mode of transport and the motorcycle was the choice of today?

CYCLE & MOTOR CYCLE SHOW
OLYMPIA   NOVEMBER 10 - 15 TH
WEST KENSINGTON — HAMMERSMITH OR ADDISON RD STATION

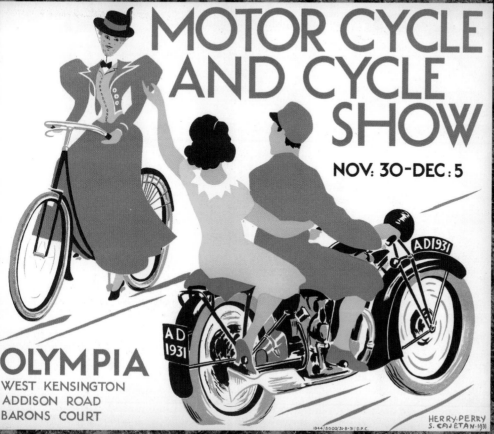

MOTOR CYCLE
AND CYCLE
SHOW

NOV: 30-DEC: 5

OLYMPIA
WEST KENSINGTON
ADDISON ROAD
BARONS COURT

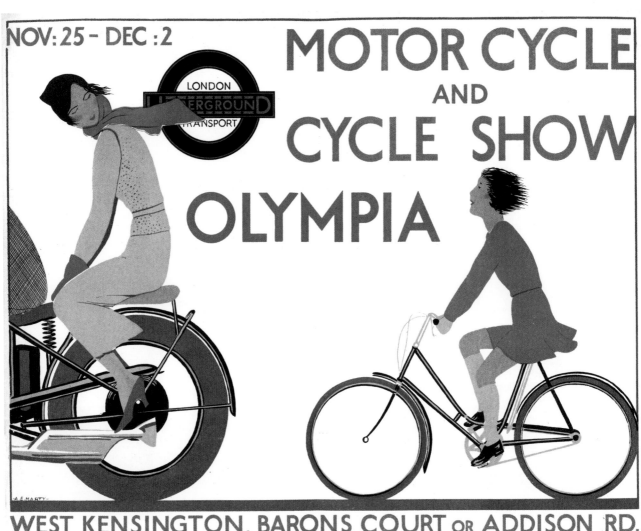

Motor Cycle and Cycle Show, by André Edouard Marty, 1933
Whilst this poster just like the one by Herry Perry shows the woman riding pillion on the motor-bike, Marty has cleverly cropped the image to exclude the presumably male driver.

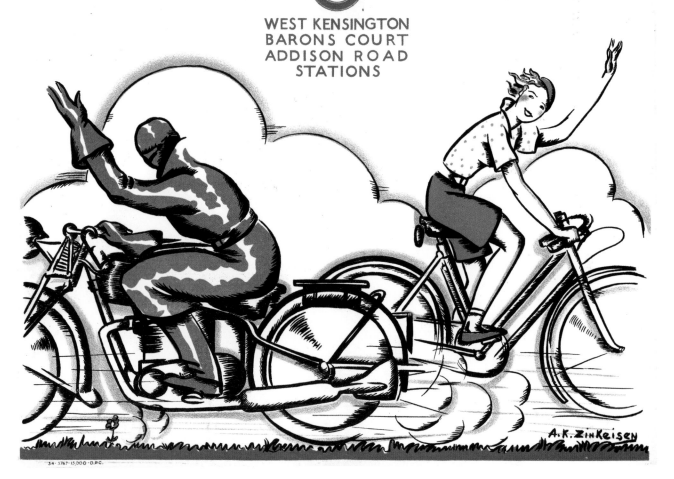

MOTOR CYCLE AND CYCLE SHOW
OLYMPIA · LONDON TRANSPORT · NOV. 5-10

WEST KENSINGTON
BARONS COURT
ADDISON ROAD
STATIONS

A·K·ZINKEISEN

34·3767·15,000·D.P.C.

Motor Cycle and Cycle Show, by Anna Zinkeisen, 1934
Continuing the theme from previous years of women on wheels, Anna Zinkeissen has evoked a
feeling of vehicles passing at speed in the open country.

Bicycle and Motorcycle Show, by Edward McKnight Kauffer, 1935
The American, McKnight Kauffer was one of England's leading poster designers but, apart from the wording, there is nothing in the design of this poster to instantly suggest a Bicycle and Motorcycle Show. It is also worth noting that by 1935 London Transport was using these posters not just to advertise its Underground Services to Olympia but also bus and coach travel to the event.

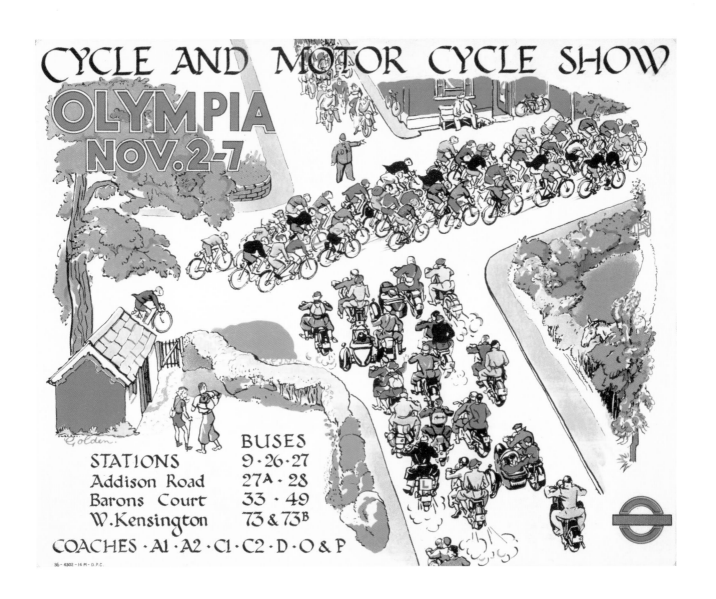

Cycle and Motor Cycle Show, by Grace Lydia Golden, 1936
Note the 'L' plate on the back of one of the motorcycles. Driving tests had only been
introduced two years earlier in 1934. Before then, although a driving licence was needed, there
was no requirement for a driving test.

Pantomimes and Circuses

These two subjects, pantomimes and circuses, are considered together in this book as in the 1950s they always appeared on the same panel poster. The reason for this is that they were both popular Christmas entertainments and thus would appeal to the same audience. Indeed, since the first pictorial poster in 1908 pantomimes have rarely justified their own poster. The Underground issued its first poster advertising London's theatreland as far back as 1909 and from then onwards it has issued a large number of colourful pictorial posters on the theme of London's theatres, a few of which also included pantomimes. In 1913 the first Underground poster appeared advertising just pantomimes. This was by the noted children's artist Mabel Lucie Attwell and was called "We're off to the Pantomime". It was the only Underground poster to advertise just pantomimes and nothing else. Much later in 1933 the first circus poster was issued. This was followed in 1936 by another very large, striking poster showing a clown's face by Barnet Freedman and then two panel posters in 1937 and 1938.

During and after the Second World War London Transport needed to concentrate first on running its services in wartime conditions and then on rebuilding a system rundown through war damage and lack of investment. Therefore, it was not until the late 1940s and early 1950s that London Transport began to advertise leisure travel once more. Post-war Britain was very different from pre-war and wartime Britain. This is reflected in the style of the posters illustrated here. Few of the noted poster designers commissioned before the war continued to make their mark on London Transport's posters after the war. New artists were commissioned for a new look and new subjects. Of course there were exceptions to prove the rule. Although the popularity of circuses has since diminished, pantomimes are still a very popular form of entertainment, but in the 1950s both pantomimes and circuses were still extremely popular family entertainment, particularly in the Christmas and New Year period. It was not until the 1950s that London Transport decided to use the small panel poster format to advertise them. By then London Transport poster output was only a shadow of its former self, but nevertheless for a few years in the 1950s London Transport did issue an annual panel poster jointly advertising these two popular forms of Christmas entertainment. However, they did not last to the end of the decade as the number of posters issued decreased even further and 1957 saw the last panel poster on these two subjects being issued.

Bertram Mills' Circus and Fun Fair, by Brian Robb, 1937
From the 1920s Bertram Mills' Circus became a popular and well known annual Christmas fixture at Olympia and was occasionally advertised on London Transport's posters. After the war, posters advertising the circus would not mention Bertram Mills' or any other circus by name. This was the first of three panel posters designed by the otherwise prolific Robb in the later 1930s, his only work for London Transport.

Pantomimes and Circuses, by Alistair Grant, 1952
This is the only poster for London Transport by Alistair Grant. Many examples of his other work
are in museum collections worldwide.

Pantomimes and Circuses, by P Temple, 1953
Many artists like to incorporate the iconic London Transport roundel as part of the design.
Here they are used as the wheels of the unicycles.

Pantomimes and Circuses, by Joan Beales, 1954
The caged animal in the centre of the poster looks more like a cat than a tiger, apart that is from its stripes. This may have been a deliberate choice on behalf of the artist since as a cat it would be linked to pantomimes but as a tiger it would represent the then popular performing animals to be seen at most circuses.

Parks and Gardens

London is very fortunate in that it has some of the best parks and gardens any city can offer. Many have long histories dating back centuries and as London's population grew and development encroached on the surrounding countryside, these parks and gardens survived and were opened to the public. They range from the neatly manicured grounds to be found at, for example, Kew Gardens or Regent's Park to the wilder and less kempt Richmond or Bushy parks with their herds of red and fallow deer. With such a wide choice of open spaces to choose from London Transport was never short of choice when deciding on which destination to choose for its posters. On some of the posters the names of several parks are listed, clearly stating which of the many parks or gardens they were meant to be advertising. By far the most popular of these parks and gardens, judging by the number of posters issued, was Kew Gardens. Regent's Park, itself, did not appear on many posters but London Zoo, which is situated within the park, appeared on the posters about the same number of times as Kew Gardens. Most of London's parks could be reached quite easily by bus, Tube or tram, although, as can be seen, not all of the posters to these parks suggested any particular mode of transport. This was for the practical reason that there were multiple different ways to reach most of these parks unlike some of the other attractions to be seen on the posters. On some of the posters, such as those advertising bluebell time, there would be no particular destination mentioned and many of these could equally apply to either London's parks or the surrounding countryside. It did not really matter which as their message to the travelling public was the same. In short it was simply to encourage Londoners to get out of doors so that they could see and enjoy the countryside or parks for themselves. From the mid-1920s until the outbreak of the Second World War the panel poster was the favoured, but by no means only, medium used to advertise the ephemeral seasonal delights of London's parks and gardens with bluebell time, crocus time and Chestnut Sunday being by far the most popular subjects. With the exception of the panel poster showing the Peter Pan statue, only the panel posters for Chestnut Sunday depicted a recognisable location as all the others are stylised views of the flowers and countryside and could be almost anywhere in or around London.

St James's Park, Hyde Park, Kew Gardens and Regents Park,
by Walter E Spradbery, 1929

OPPOSITE:
See London's Parks and Rivers, by Zero (Hans Schleger), 1938
Apart from the River Thames, which rivers was this poster referring to?
Fortunately the River Wandle and River Lea both survive but most of London's former rivers such
as the Fleet, Effra and Westbourne are now buried underground.

Bee about, Anonymous, 1938
After the evening rush hour was over there was spare capacity on the company's fleet of trams
and trolleybuses. To try and fill this space 6d evening tourist tickets were issued for use only on
the trolleybus and tram network.

Tea on the lawn at Alexandra Palace,
by Kraber (John Roland Barker) 1939
Although Wood Green station, the nearest to Alexandra Palace, opened in 1932 it was not until
1939 that London Transport issued its first pictorial poster to advertise attractions at Alexandra
Palace, and then it was only as a car card advertising tea on the lawn. Previously most of the
company's advertising for Alexandra Palace had been for its much more direct tram services.
Unlike this poster these typographic posters, which could be seen posted on the company's tram
poles, listed the various activities such as dancing, roller skating or concerts and not the grounds.

SEE LONDON'S PARKS AND RIVERS

BEE ABOUT

6ᵈ evening tourist tickets after 6 p.m.

TEA ON THE LAWN AT *alexandra palace*

BLUEBELLS!

KEW GARDENS UNDERGROUND

Bluebell Time, by André Edouard Marty, 1933
Seasonal changes were a good excuse to encourage off peak use of the system.

OPPOSITE:
Bluebells! Kew Gardens, by Fawkes, 1930
Unlike the more generic mentions of "Bluebell Time", the Fawkes poster actively promotes a single destination for flora adoration.

Bluebell Time, by Herry Perry, 1931
On this delightful poster it was felt that there was no need to tell people where they should go to see the bluebells or indeed that they should travel by Underground or bus. As this panel poster would be displayed inside the company's trains it was enough just to imprint the idea on the passenger's mind that it was now time to see the bluebells.

Crocus Time, by Herry Perry, 1931
Unlike the posters advertising "Bluebell Time" which often mentioned no particular
destination, those advertising "Crocus Time" always listed a choice of London's parks for
people to visit. Although the choice of these varied over the years it always included
Kew Gardens,

Crocus Time, by André Edouard Marty, 1933
This poster, together with another issued the following year advertising "Bluebell Time",
unintentionally gave out the wrong message as it shows a young girl picking the wild flowers.
This was addressed in 1935 when some posters on the same theme carried lines such as
"Leave them for others to see" or "Please don't pull them".

Crocus Time, by Anna Zinkeisen, 1934
Anna Zinkeisen's depiction of the famous Peter Pan Statue in Kensington Gardens (one of the destinations listed on the poster) is instantly recognisable. J M Barrie, the creator of Peter Pan, commissioned Sir George Frampton to make the bronze statue which has graced the gardens since 1912. The crocus clad hills surrounding the statue are a figment of the artist's imagination.

Crocus Time, by Herry Perry, 1935
Between 1927 and 1938 Herry Perry was commissioned to design over fifty posters first for the Underground and then London Transport, far outstripping any other woman artist in the number of posters she designed.

TO BUSHEY PARK   BY TRAM
FROM HAMMERSMITH WIMBLEDON OR SHEPHERDS BUSH STATIONS

UNDERGROUND

D·M·BATTY   1 9 2 7

CHESTNUT   SUNDAY

BUSHEY PARK
By Tram from Hammersmith, Wimbledon, or Shepherds Bush Stations.

Chestnut Sunday, Bushy Park, by Charles Burton, 1930

Bushy Park, sometimes incorrectly spelled Bushey on 1920s Underground posters, is London's second largest park and was for many years famous for its magnificent avenue of chestnut trees which was planted in the late 17th century after Sir Christopher Wren conceived the idea of the mile-long Chestnut Avenue as a formal approach to Hampton Court Palace. The park was opened to the public by Queen Victoria and soon became very popular. Particularly fine were the displays of chestnut blossoms in late spring and the tradition of parading down Chestnut Avenue on the Sunday closest to 11th May (when the blossoms are said to be at their finest) began. Even the royal family took part in Chestnut Sunday. Chestnut Sunday was suspended during both World Wars. After the Second World War it was not held again until the tradition restarted in 1977, the year of the Queen's Jubilee. Although Bushy Park was well served by the Southern Railway no Underground trains ran out this far. However, the company's trams and buses did reach Hampton Court and bus excursions were also laid on for the day.

OPPOSITE:
To Bushey Park by tram, by David Wilson, 1926

With the incorrect spelling the poster simply extols the virtues of a bright summer's Bushy day.

Chestnut Sunday, by Dora M Batty, 1927

Batty's work, always rich in symbolism, uses only hands embracing chestnut tree flowers.

CHESTNUT SUNDAY
BUSHY PARK

HERRY-PERRY, Lent 1931

BUSHY PARK

CHESTNUT SUNDAY

UNDERGROUND

A.E. MARTY

Chestnut Sunday, Bushy Park, by Herry Perry, 1935

In contrast to her 1931 poster of couples and families enjoying a stroll along the busy avenue of chestnut trees her poster for 1935 shows a deserted avenue apart, that is, from the two children in the foreground.

OPPOSITE:

Chestnut Sunday, by Herry Perry, 1931

A common element to be found in several of Herry Perry's 1931 posters is a pigeon wearing a hat. See her posters for Bluebell Time, Crocus Time, Chestnut Sunday and the RAF Display shown elsewhere in the book.

Bushy Park, Chestnut Sunday, by André Edouard Marty, 1933

Marty, who is best known for his work in fashion magazines such as Vogue, Harper's Bazaar and Vanity Fair, was also on the jury for the 1925 *Exposition International des Arts Décoratifs et Industries Modernes* from which the Art Deco movement took its name. Regardless of subject, the common theme running throughout all his Underground panel posters is his inclusion of an elegant young woman and child.

RAF Displays

From its earliest days Hendon, in north London, has played an important part in Britain's aviation history and can be considered London's first airport. As early as September 1911 the first official UK airmail was flown between Hendon and Windsor as part of the celebrations of the coronation of King George V. A year later in 1912, the first Aerial Derby which circumnavigated around and just beyond the outer London suburbs started and ended at Hendon. This spectacular event was viewed by approximately three million people across London, most of whom had probably never seen an aircraft fly before. These annual events which were advertised on Underground posters as early as 1913 became as important fixtures as the Ascot and Epsom races in the London calendar. The importance of Hendon grew yet again when during the First World War, in November 1916, the War Office took over the flying schools located there, training 490 pilots. Although it would then be some years after the war, in 1922, that the first RAF "Pageant" was held it was not until the following year in 1923 that the Underground commissioned Aldo Cosomati to produce its first poster to advertise this new RAF Display. In 1922 Hendon Aerodrome was not particularly conveniently situated for the Underground as the nearest station was still Golders Green. This meant that until the Northern Line extension was built passengers were advised to travel to Golders Green by Underground "and thence by bus" to the Aerodrome. The following year Hendon Central station became the end of the Northern Line with the final extension to Colindale and Edgware opening two months after the Pageant thus allowing the much more conveniently located Colindale station to be used. The Pageant soon established itself as a regular event, and with a change of name in 1925 it was to become known as the Royal Air Force Display. In that year over 100,000 people saw the event at Hendon. A few years later in 1938 it was renamed yet again to become The Empire Air Day. Throughout the 1930s these attractive panel posters were the main method the Underground and later London Transport used to advertise the event to Londoners, few of whom would still ever have travelled by plane or maybe even regularly have seen one flying over the City. There can be little doubt the novelty of flying along with patriotism helped to increase the popularity of the RAF Pageants at Hendon.

RAF Display, by Charles Burton, 1930
This view of a boy with his grounded kite looking wistfully at the overhead planes could almost
be a recruiting poster for the next generation of RAF pilots.

RAF Display June 27th, by Herry Perry, 1931
Unlike the other posters advertising the RAF display at Hendon shown here, Herry Perry's poster concentrates on the spectators looking skyward towards an invisible plane. Many of Perry's posters have a comic or humorous element. Here as in several of her other 1931 posters she includes a pigeon wearing a hat and carrying a cane, looking up to the planes flying out of sight overhead.

RAF Display, by Dora M Batty, 1932
In the 1920s and 30s Dora Batty was one of the leading woman poster designers working for the Underground. The other was Herry Perry whose work also appears in this book. Batty is also known for her designs for Poole Pottery, as well as publicity work for MacFisheries. Between 1932 and 1958 Batty was a Tutor in the Textiles Department at the Central School of Arts And Crafts, London and in the 1940s she also taught Fabric Design and Illustration at Camberwell School of Art.

RAF Display, by André Edouard Marty, 1933

To the modern eye there appears to be a strong contrast between the fashionable elegance of the lady watching the massed planes flying directly towards her and the aircraft which, being bi-planes, appear rather antiquated or old fashioned. However, it must be remembered that in 1933 bi-planes were still the most common type of aircraft in use by the RAF, with the final type being introduced into service four years later in 1937.

RAF Display, Anna Zinkeisen, 1934
Compared to the planes in Marty's poster the previous year these streamlined monoplanes
suggest great speed and modernity, yet by the following year biplanes were again depicted on
the RAF Display posters.

RAF Display, by Zero (Hans Schleger), 1935
The air display was filled with activities, which must have thrilled all those watching. In this poster
a parachutist is shown floating to the ground, but this was not the most exciting part of the show
to be seen at Hendon, as one of the activities was a bombing run with live ammunition.

Rugby

Although there are several rugby grounds spread out around the capital, until the Second World War London Transport only ever issued one pictorial poster to advertise these many club grounds. This was in 1935. Instead of regularly appearing on a pictorial poster London's rugby matches would be advertised on posters with titles such as "This week in London". These posters listed a whole variety of sporting events, exhibitions and concerts, including rugby. The Underground's first ever pictorial poster to advertise rugby in London was Laura Knight's striking "Rugby at Twickenham" poster. This was issued in 1921 and with no Underground station at Twickenham passengers were instructed to complete their journey onward from Shepherd's Bush or Hammersmith by tram. Although this poster advertised rugby at Twickenham it does not appear to have been produced to advertise a particular match. It was not until 1927 that another poster, this time with a photographic image, was issued to advertise another match at Twickenham. This match was between England and Wales.

Neither version of rugby has ever been as popular as football in London but in 1929, in an attempt to increase its popularity outside of its northern heartland, the Rugby League Cup Final was played at Wembley Stadium and it was an outstanding success. Over 41,500 spectators turned out to watch the match. Unlike Twickenham, Wembley Stadium was well served by many stations including Wembley, Wembley Park, Alperton, Wembley Hill and Wembley Stadium (LNER), not to mention trams and buses, so for most Londoners it was easy to reach. It was only then, with the Rugby League Cup Final at Wembley, that the Underground began to issue an annual poster for this sport. These posters were presumably printed before the names of the teams were known as none of the teams is listed on the posters, unlike those advertising matches at Twickenham in which both teams were usually named. All of these posters advertising the Rugby League Cup Final at Wembley were in the small panel format, whereas the smaller number of poster issued advertising Twickenham also included a number of the much larger double royal size. As with many sporting events the Second World War saw a temporary end to rugby's Cup Final at Wembley. It did not return until 1946. With rugby back at Wembley it might have been expected that London Transport would once again have produced posters advertising the match but it did not, although a couple of posters were issued listing London's rugby grounds and how to get there.

Rugby League Cup Final, by Charles Burton, 1930
In this, as in the other posters, the players shown do not depict the two teams. They are wearing the wrong kit for it to be Halifax and York which participated in that year's final.

OPPOSITE:
Rugby League Cup Final, by Herry Perry, 1933
It would have been more helpful to passengers to make clear that Wembley Park was close to the Stadium. Wembley Central is about a mile away. This poster includes a very unusual use of a half roundel.

Rugby League Cup Final, by Anna Zinkeisen, 1934
Two very different parts of the game are successfully captured in these two contrasting posters, both by women artists.

Rugby League Final, by Herry Perry, 1935
In 1935 London Transport must have had a change of policy because now, rather than just saying travel by Underground this, and other posters, began listing *all* the routes to Wembley, including by the rival operator the London & North Eastern Railway (LNER).

All Blacks at Twickenham, by Hyman Segal, 1935
Segal was born in London in 1914 and attended the Jew's Free School in Camden Town, from where, aged 12, he won a scholarship to St. Martin's School of Art. His iconic image of an All Blacks player carrying the ball towards the line appears to be Segal's only poster for London Transport.

RUGBY LEAGUE FINAL
WEMBLEY STADIUM   APRIL 18   3 P.M.

Stations-Wembley; Wembley Park; Alperton, thence bus 83; or Wembley Hill or Wembley Stadium (L.N.E.R.)   Buses 18, 18c, 83   Trams 28, 62

Rugby League Final, by Tom Eckersley and Eric Lombers, 1936
Tom Eckersley and Eric Lombers met at art school in Salford, and in 1934 they moved to London where they soon established their careers. Together they produced 38 posters for London Transport, 15 of them for panels. The partnership ended at the outbreak of the Second World War. After the war Tom Eckersley continued to design many more posters alone for London Transport – some shown in this book – his last being in 1995.

OPPOSITE:
Rugby League Cup Final, by Gill Lancaster, 1937
Nothing is known about Gill Lancaster, who only produced three designs for London Transport, all in 1937. One for cricket is shown elsewhere in this book.

Trooping the Colour

The custom of Trooping the Colour originally had a very important purpose and dates to the 17th Century when the Colours of a regiment were used as a rallying point in battle and were trooped in front of the soldiers every day to ensure that each soldier could recognise those of his own regiment. This was done in London by the Foot Guards as part of their daily Guard Mounting on Horse Guards and the modern Trooping the Colour parade is still carried out along similar lines. The first record of the monarch's birthday being honoured by the Grenadier Guards was in 1748 but it was not until George III became King in 1760, that it was ordered that parades should mark the King's Birthday. Since the reign of George IV they have become, with a few exceptions, such as both World Wars, an annual event.

This impressive and colourful display of pageantry is nowadays almost always held in June, on the occasion of the Queen's Official Birthday. It has for many years been televised live and although there is no need to visit Horse Guards Parade to see it as it happens it still attracts huge crowds. The ceremony is carried out by the monarch's personal troops, the Household Division, on Horse Guards Parade, with the monarch taking the salute.

Subject to necessary operational commitments the regiments take their turn to be part of this historic display. It is always an impressive sight with over 1000 soldiers on parade, along with their horses and military bands. For those unable to gain access to Horse Guards Parade to see the main event the parade can be watched as it travels from Buckingham Palace along The Mall to Horse Guards Parade, Whitehall and back.

The Underground Group issued its first posters to encourage Londoners to travel to the Trooping the Colour from 1912 to 1914 and then, with the event cancelled for the duration of the First World War, it was not until 1922 that the Underground again issued an almost annual pictorial poster. These were almost exclusively in the small panel format shown here. The outbreak of the Second World War saw the ceremony cancelled again and although it restarted once more in 1947 it was not until 1952 that London Transport began again to issue the occasional poster advertising the event. Then on the 1st June 1955 the Trooping of the Colour was again cancelled when a National Emergency was called as a result of a Railway Strike, but by then with just over a week to go the panel poster had been printed.

TROOPING THE COLOUR

JUNE 3RD 1925

NEAREST UNDERGROUND STATIONS

TRAFALGAR SQUARE, CHARING CROSS or St JAMES'S PARK

TROOPING THE COLOUR JUNE 3rd

NEAREST STATIONS

St JAMES PK _ TRAFALGAR SQ _ STRAND _ WESTMINSTER

Within the poster:

HERRY·PERRY
S MARK'S EVE
1931

TROOPING
THE
COLOUR

HORSE GUARDS PARADE

JUNE 6

ST JAMES
PARK STATION

1030/8,000/6·5·31. D.P.C.

Trooping the Colour, by Herry Perry, 1931
Between 1927 and 1938 Herry Perry was commissioned to design over fifty posters first for the
Underground and then London Transport, far outstripping any other woman artist.
When signing and dating her posters Herry Perry often added a saint's day to the date. This poster
is dated St Mark's Eve (24th April) which is the day before the feast day of St Mark the Evangelist.

OPPOSITE:
Trooping the Colour, by L B Black, 1925
Black utilises the symmetry of a uniformed military parade to great effect here. The Charing Cross
and Strand stations mentioned in this and the second poster are today named Embankment and
Charing Cross respectively.

Trooping the Colour, by Charles Burton, 1930
1930 was the second year King George V was prevented by illness from attending so this year the
salute was taken by the Prince of Wales.

Trooping the Colour, by André Edouard Marty, 1933
Once again Marty focuses on the woman and child spectators, rather than the soldiers in the parade which they are watching.

OPPOSITE:
Trooping the Colour, by Anna Zinkeisen, 1934

Trooping the Colour, by Dora M Batty, 1936
Due to his abdication in November of that year this was the only time that King Edward VIII attended the event.

STATION MARBLE ARCH
OR HYDE PARK CORNER
OR BY BUS OR COACH

PRESENTATION
of COLOURS *by*
H·M·THE KING

HYDE
PARK
JULY 16

Presentation of Colours by HM the King, by Dora M Batty, 1936

When he was Prince of Wales, Edward joined the Grenadier Guards in 1914 to serve in World War One, and reached the rank of Captain in 1916. When he acceded to the throne in January 1936 he was appointed Colonel-in-Chief of the five regiments of Foot Guards and so it was to be expected that he would present the new colours. This ceremony should not be confused with Trooping The Colour which took place the previous month. One notable incident which occurred after the parade in Hyde Park was when a man in the crowd, called McMahon, tried to shoot the King but was prevented, and arrested.

Trooping the Colour, by Stephen Green, 1955
This year the parade was cancelled due to a rail strike but the poster had already been printed.

Wimbledon

It may surprise many to learn that when Wimbledon was founded in 1868, what is now officially the "All England Lawn Tennis and Croquet Club" did not originally include tennis as one of its activities or even in its title. Tennis was only added in 1876 and the first tennis championship was held the following year. This makes it the oldest championship in the world and the only Grand Slam still to play on grass. However, it was not until 1922 when the club moved a short distance to its current location in Church Road that the Underground started to commission pictorial posters to advertise the championship. It is not certain but probably the change in venue played a part in this decision as the new venue was now closer to the District Line.

Even so for those wishing to travel to watch the tennis Wimbledon Tennis Club was not, by Londoner's standards, particularly convenient for the Underground with only the District Line branch from Earls Court to Wimbledon running relatively nearby. When on the 13th September 1926 the Northern Line's South Wimbledon station opened it was even less suited for those travelling to watch the tennis as it was over twice the distance as Southfields at almost two miles away. So this is why most of the posters instructed passengers to travel by the District Line to Southfields. Spectators who travelled via Southfields station could then catch a special bus to the grounds. This was not usually the case if travelling via South Wimbledon as the posters normally only mentioned onwards travel by bus, meaning the regular service bus rather than a special service to the tennis grounds. Just down the line from Southfields station was the District Line's terminus at Wimbledon. This station was a major interchange with the Southern Railway's mainline from Portsmouth to London Waterloo. As was to be expected no mention was made of travel by this rival company's trains to and from London even though the buses from South Wimbledon would pass directly in front of the station. However on match days the Underground did lay on extra District Line trains to help cope with the crowds and connect with the fleet of special buses which ran every two or three minutes. In addition to encouraging travel by the Underground the Underground Group also produced a number of letterpress posters promoting travel from the suburbs by the company's trams and trolleybuses to Wimbledon.

LAWN TENNIS CHAMPIONSHIP MEETING
AT WIMBLEDON — UNDERGROUND TO SOUTH WIMBLEDON Stn
FROM JUNE 25TH THENCE BY SPECIAL BUS.

WIMBLEDON

FROM JUNE 23rd

SOUTH WIMBLEDON
STATION
THENCE BY BUS

Wimbledon, by Herry Perry, 1931
This poster, in which the ball boy dominates the foreground, shows a Mixed Doubles match,
which along with the Ladies Doubles, was added in 1913.

OPPOSITE:
Lawn Tennis Championship Meeting, by Percy Drake Brookshaw, 1928
This appears to have been the only year in which the Underground advertised a special bus
service from South Wimbledon station to the tennis grounds.

Wimbledon, by Charles Burton, 1930
Depicting the sport as the height of chic, Burton chose a sole stylish player in somewhat
pointier shoes than would perhaps be suitable for such an energetic game

Wimbledon Tennis, by André Edouard Marty, 1933
To his oft-used theme of female and child spectator, Marty adds the players' customary sporting
handshake to proceedings.

Wimbledon Tennis, by Anna Zinkeisen, 1934

Whilst the subject of this poster cannot be in doubt there is something unnatural about the image. With her right leg extended it appears as if the contestant is a ballerina standing en pointe rather than a tennis player in a match at Wimbledon. In addition, the oddly positioned aerial view of the Centre Court makes it look as though it is floating in air.

Wimbledon Tennis, by Herry Perry, 1935
Perry's love of the airbrushing technique and her liberal adaptation of the Johnston lettering
(her letter U for example) are much in evidence here.

OPPOSITE:
Davis Cup, Wimbledon, by Walter Goetz, 1936
In some years other major tennis tournaments were held at Wimbledon. These saw just four
London Transport posters issued from 1934 to 1937 to advertise travel to the Davis Cup and one
(not illustrated here) for the women's Wightman Cup which was held in London on alternate years.

Wimbledon Championships, by Tom Eckersley and Eric Lombers, 1937
No mistaking the subject matter here: the artists' piercing clarity is on the tools of the sport.

DAVIS CUP WIMBLEDON

Interzone Final – July 18, 20 & 21
Challenge Round – July 25, 27 & 28

STATION – SOUTHFIELDS thence by special bus to the ground

WIMBLEDON CHAMPIONSHIPS

FROM JUNE 21 TO JULY 3

BY UNDERGROUND TO SOUTHFIELDS
THENCE SPECIAL BUS TO THE GROUND

Zoo

Nowadays, zoos may have fallen out of favour but in the mid-twentieth century they were still at the height of their popularity as a family day out, none more so than London Zoo. So it is not surprising that, due to its popularity and possibly also its colourful and exotic subject matter, London Transport issued more pictorial posters advertising travel to London Zoo than to any other single destination (with the exception of Kew Gardens). However, when the Zoo first opened in 1826 only members of the Zoological Society of London were allowed to visit: the public were not allowed in until 1847. London Zoo is situated along the northern edge of Regent's Park and not particularly easily accessible by Underground train. The closet station is not, as one might expect, Regent's Park station which is over one mile away but Camden Town, still a surprising three-quarters of a mile from the Zoo. This is why over the years the Underground's, and later London Transport's, posters suggested six different stations as the best way to reach the Zoo. Camden Town (the nearest) appeared the most often, followed some way behind by Regent's Park. The other stations were Chalk Farm, Baker Street and St John's Wood, which was renamed Lord's for less than one year before closing due to the war. Another station at Mornington Crescent was, at under one mile away, still closer than some of these other stations. However, as it was on the same line as the closest, Camden Town, and also for many years closed at weekends, its name never appeared on the pictorial posters. The Underground's first poster advertising the Zoo appeared in 1913, with the next in 1915. Then, from 1920 until the outbreak of the Second World War, each year saw at least one or more posters advertising the different delights and attractions of the Zoo, not to mention other posters advertising Whipsnade (via Green Line Coach). But of the sixty-plus posters advertising London Zoo only a relatively small number were in this small panel format. As with many of the other themes illustrated in this book these panel posters advertising the Zoo were usually used to highlight special events, for example late night openings or the presence of a particularly popular or unusual animal such as the giant panda, Komodo dragon or lion cubs.

The Zoo by Floodlight, by Tom Eckersley and Eric Lombers, 1935
The Zoo's popularity was so great in the 1930s that it experimented with late evening openings.
At first this was just on Thursdays but it soon expanded to two nights a week. These came to an
end when the Zoo closed at the outbreak of World War Two (although they have recently been
reinstated by ZSL). This poster was one of the first to be designed by the successful partnership
of Tom Eckersley and Eric Lombers.

Zoo Nights, by Clifford Ellis and Rosemary Ellis, 1936
In this poster the husband and wife team of Clifford and Rosemary Ellis chose an
anthropomorphic theme of elegantly dressed animals to advertise the London Zoo's
late night openings.

Zoo Nights, by Harry Blacker, 1939
This was one of only two posters designed by Harry Blacker for London Transport. Both were in this format. Although he was a successful commercial illustrator Blacker is perhaps better known as the cartoonist Nero. Lords station was replaced by the one at St John's Wood later in 1939.

Giant Panda, by Clifford Ellis and Rosemary Ellis, 1939
Ming was London Zoo's and Britain's first ever giant panda cub and soon became a
national celebrity. Not long after this poster was issued shortly before the outbreak of the
war she was transferred to Whipsnade where she joined her older siblings Tang and Sung.
During the war she made several return visits to London Zoo but sadly died in 1944.

Bibliography

Bownes, David and Green, Oliver, London Transport Posters, Lund Humphries, 2008

Dodd, John, Maps of London's Transport: Design Variety in the First Half of the
    Twentieth Century, Capital Transport, 2016

Green, Oliver, Underground Art, Laurence King, 2001

Green, Oliver and Rewse-Davies, Jeremy, Designed for London, Laurence King, 1995

Hutchison, Harold, London Transport Posters, London Transport Board, 1963

Laver, James and Hutchison, Harold, Art for All, Art and Technics, 1949

Ovenden, Mark, Johnston & Gill, Very British Types, Lund Humphries, 2016

Ovenden, Mark, London Underground by Design, Penguin, 2013

Riddell, Jonathan, Pleasure Trips by Underground, Capital Transport, 1998

Riddell, Jonathan and Denton, Peter, By Underground to the Zoo, Studio Vista, 1995

Riddell, Jonathan and Stearn, William T, By Underground to Kew, Studio Vista, 1994

Rose, Doug, The London Underground – A Diagrammatic History, 9th edition, 2016